T0128242

CONSECRATION
and CELEBRATION

A COLLECTION OF POEMS

Temitope Oshin

WESTBOW
P R E S S®
A DIVISION OF THOMAS NELSON
& ZONDERVAN

WestBow Press books may be ordered through booksellers or by contacting:

WestBow Press
A Division of Thomas Nelson & Zondervan
1663 Liberty Drive
Bloomington, IN 47403
www.westbowpress.com
1 (866) 928-1240

ISBN: 978-1-9736-3202-3 (sc)
ISBN: 978-1-9736-3201-6 (e)

Print information available on the last page.

WestBow Press rev. date: 8/2/2018

DEDICATION

This work is dedicated
"To God my Exceeding Joy"
(Psalm 43:4)
"My Father ... the Guide of my youth" (Jeremiah 3:4)

ACKNOWLEDGEMENTS

"…The good works of some are clearly evident…" (1Timothy 5: 25)

Clearly evident, and in magnanimous ways contributing to the success of this anthology, are the kind support I received from my family and friends. Dr. Wale Oshin, Adeola Onichabor, Taiwo Adebayo, Kehinde Oshin, Dare Forte and Abimbola Sowemimo. Thank you all. I appreciate your good gifts. Thank you for your confidence in me.

CONTENTS

POEMS OF CONSECRATION

POEMS ON CHRISTIAN SERVICE

POEMS ON CHARACTER

OF WHAT USE IS IT?

Of what use is a branded stick
Which gets you sick?
Of what use is that "lethal leaf"
Which leaves you bereft of your healthy self?
Of what use is that "medicinal legume"
Which ends up to consume?

Of what use is a product
Which harms you and your duct?
Of what use is the pipe
Which makes you always gripe?
Of what use is that offensive plume source
Which, like pores, leaks your purse;
Whose obnoxious smoke drenches
And leaves you in its unpleasant "stenches"?

Of what use are cigarettes
Which leave you with an addict's regrets
Of what use is tobacco's oomph
Which makes you to back homely roof?
Of what use are hard drugs
Which gives you façade of thugs?

Of what use is heroin
Which puts out a shining hero or heroine?
Of what use is that narcotic
Whose aberrant use makes you eccentric?
Of what use is marijuana
Which gives you a phony "merry" mania?

1

Of what use is that "weed"
Whose end is to leave you in calamitous need?

Of what use is cocaine
Which reduces the brain to a flopping bane?

Several peasants, many greats and nobles
Are stumbled by "it" and vexed by its troubles
Here today, a little smoky puff
There tomorrow, another diminutive "stuff"
Putting them in a depressive plight
Oh what a number there are: many gifted and bright!

Of what use is "it", dear reader,
That for which woes await the impenitent user:
Heightened hysteria, fiery frenzy, pitch-black paunch?
Discontinue "it"! Use and abuse, staunch!

CRACK OR LACK

A neglected foible
Makes character crumble
If you've got a lack—
Fill it
If you have a crack—
Fix it
For little flaws
Engender fatal falls

Curb it now
Don't cuddle it
Nib it in the bud now
Don't nurture it
Face your foes now
And phase them out
For internal foes
Might become external woes

THE LIVING CODE

Get your code of living
From the Source that's Living
Not from a human being

It's sad to see today
Big men in big mess
Stars with moral scars
Celebrities without integrity

There's Solution
In God's Absolution
If all will seek Him right
His Word guides aright
Stars and celebrities alike

POEMS ON CHARITY AND LOVE

- Edu-Caution!
- Marriage
- A Musical Discourse

EDU-CAUTION!

It begins at home for majority
Lessons, blessings and warnings
Father's fretful calls and chidings
Mother's mild counsel on chastity

Aloud they gleam from them:
The parents and adults in their dwelling
Wise words from 'Ma and 'Pa to steer their youthful realm
Yet the adults' "loud" behaviour is ingrained without any
    inkling

At home is a type of learning—
Education without the blackboard and chalk
Yet with curriculum too broad for formal talk
Adolescents' erudition comes with observation of many

Unconscious Education it is for the young,
Concerted "Edu-caution" it should be for the old
Teenagers grasp, imitate and make out a life-mould
From the "untaught" lessons their heroes sing

The media is another classroom they know
Studded artistes, decorated singers from the tube's daily
    glow
Teaching modern manners, often with offensive excesses,
Readily sponged by the adolescent's mind's recesses

Unsuspecting, unguided and callow youngsters
In need of the guiding light of moral stars

Duty calls on all to educate them aright
By positive verbal instructions and unvoiced acts

Education continues with their peers
Habits copied, colloquialisms collocated
Manners mimicked and mannerisms mirrored
From equally naive friends—their un-tutored "teachers"

Some may find out that not all pals pass
For followership, neither do all actors and stars;
A few unguided ones live with the gathered "un-character"
    codswallop—
An avoidable fate if the "experienced educators", of their
    duty, are atop

Edu-caution: A word for the grown-up guides!
Be vigilant with your represented values
With militant meticulousness as mentors
Educate with caution; your actions are being mirrored!

Marriage

The man is the head
She shall not stand in his stead
In the Word of the Lord it is said
"The husband is the head
Of the wife, as also Christ is the Head
Of the Church" true till the end

If you think that's weird
Hear what the Lord said
"A man shall leave his father and
Mother and be joined to his wife, and
The two shall become one flesh" when they wed
Now you see the union of two is blessed

Before you think that's the end
More still to know about the bed
Hear it as it was said
"Marriage is honorable among all, and
The bed undefiled"...
Warning this is my friend
You must uphold it till the end

One more light to be shed
On God's fruits for the Blessed
Union—Children must be fed
Cared for and that's not the end
"Bring them up in the training and admonition of the Lord"
the Bible said

A Musical Discourse

Rising up early and racing
To lessons for singing or playing
Amazed by your enthusing devotion
To your melodic affection

When the notes and cords begin to play
I wonder then what you'd say
When the songs are set to tune
That to happen soon

The King's high praise
To the heavens I'd raise
To His glory I'd sing
With the guitar strings

My tutorial transcends guitar cords
For to create sound relationship
You must learn to strike cordial chords
And know the limits of playing that's flip

POEMS OF CELEBRATION

WHEN IT'S TOLD

When it's told He was born in a manger,
All receive it with laughter.
When it's told He was born of a virgin,
Many still offer a grin.
When it's told He died on a cross,
It makes no one cross.
When it's told on the third day He arose,
Most argue the truth's but a ruse.

When it was told the tomb was found empty,
Many saw Him walked the city.
With His fold and friends He drank and ate,
Holes in hands and feet!
What's gold but to see the Risen Lord,
Five hundred did at once;
When sold freely to our sin-wretched world,
Earned hell's rescue for millions!

When told that old story of His victorious life
There's joy to the seeking heart.
When it's told He came to save the lost life
Redemption comes with it
When it's told God's Son seeks sons—
An invitation to all, call it
When it's told Jesus was crucified, died and rose
Rescues if you'll believe it

Happy Easter!

MORE THAN A WISH

You deserve more than a wish
Better is a prayer that is rich:

"Every way you turn
The Lord will lead you on

For each course you chart
You will find grace to start

On all that is yours
You will suffer no loss

Issues that make you whine
In no time shall be fine"

Have a day full of mirth
As you celebrate your birth

GRACE

In the coming days
May you find sufficient grace
To occupy your true place
Overcome oppositions you may face
And run to finish the race

Happy Birthday!

God's Hamper

Gifts have been exchanging hands
Some loaded in baskets or hampers
Speaking love with loud whispers--
The universal language across many lands

Once an ancient prophet was asked
What do you see Jeremiah?
One basket full of good ripe fruits and
Another full of bad ones, he replied.

God has got good basket-loads
Of blessings and promises, dear
His hamper of gifts traverses many roads
To reach you, this season, and forever.

Here the seven-fold blessings proclaimed
From that basket of good gifts:

God will set His eyes on you for good
He will bring you back to the good land
He will build you and not pull you down
He will plant you and not pluck you up
He will give you a heart to know Him as the Lord
You shall be His people and He will be your God
You shall return to Him with your whole heart.
(Jeremiah 24:6, 7)

May these blessings be yours now and always.
Merry Christmas and a Happy New Year!

JULY

As you journey through July
May you be lifted high
On new heights to fly
Where storms are bidden bye

Christ be your Guide
Day and night by your side
This month as you ride
In His love with pride

Happy New Month!

HE CAME

He came that low
Through the greatest woe
Defeating the greatest foe
In a grand slide show

His hands got the holes
For He seeks ordinary souls
Like yours to make whole
If Him you'll follow

Happy Easter!

A Great Cost

At a great cost
He sought to make just
All humanity lost

Into great joy now burst
The Saviour is risen from the grave
Sing His praise we must

That's one story
For telling we'll never be sorry
Jesus' humiliation and glory

Happy Easter!

POEMS OF CONSECRATION

- The Construction Site
- On the Altar
- Born Again
- All
- Freedom

THE CONSTRUCTION SITE

The sight at the construction site does not seem attractive
The building falls short of its potential beauty
Sand, stone and grit litter the premises
As though all are materials with no promises

The construction site...
Very busy in the day
Men, machinery and materials at work
Laying, casting and plastering –
But at night?
Lonely and deserted for the day's job to take form

At the construction site...
One stands who calls the shots:
"The Standards and nothing short!"
The Master Builder, Jesus Christ, is at work
At the construction site where He builds His own!

> "...You are **God's building**. According to **the grace of God** which was given ... as a wise master builder... for no other foundation can anyone lay than that which is laid, which is **Jesus Christ**."
> (I Corinthians 3:9, 10, 11)

ON THE ALTAR

On God's altar I offer my life
I refuse to make a flight
For to work in me His life
To the altar I must stay tight

Though it pains
Yet it pays
For much are the gains
Daily on the altar as I stay

Service offered to Christ
My life and devotion His to have
Till Him I see at last
Forever Jesus I'll serve

BORN AGAIN

Twice was my birth
Both times in mirth
The first brought
My earthly admission
The second bought
My sin's remission

Twice I was born
Once as a baby
From the womb tenderly
Then as God's son
By faith in The Son
Gracefully born again

ALL

All for my All-in-All
That's what I'm willing to give
Nothing withheld
Everything bared

For such love unheard
I'll reciprocate
Me He'll have fully
As Him I have wholly

All for You my Lord
Time, trust and more
Devotion and dedication
Consecration and all

All I ask is that One
That One thing I seek
The All-satisfying One I befriended
Whom now I seek in unlimited measure

All for You Father
All for You Jesus
More of You Friend
More of You Holy Spirit Eternal

Come in limitless measure
Fill me with Your Treasure
The Presence that makes
Then I'll be sold out to Him, my All

FREEDOM

Lord, all lying in my life
That negates Your Holy Name
Please subject to shame
And chase away like chaff
Blown away by the wind
So I would be free indeed

POEMS ON
CHRISTIAN SERVICE

- A Call from the Cliff
- No Match
- Rewards
- My Noble Vine

A Call from the Cliff

Hey, this is Me from the cliff.
I've tried reaching you severally
You've got yourself so busy, obviously
Hope this time you'd get the brief.

I need one who'd be fearless to speak
Of My love to the whiz kids and profs.
However shallow your knowledge's troughs
You'd be My genius if you make this stick

Would you come up right away?
I am out of men on this **ivory tower**
They have failed the major of their stay
Leaving the kids in darkness to waste and wander

Atop here, I've got no light
Hope you'd finish up down there sooner
And be My torch shining bright
I have your table set on this **corporate tower**

Many I called up have gone on AWOL
By the busyness and bossiness of the black suit.
How soon they'd forgotten their Root
On gaining the world now losing their souls!

Come up this **watchtower**
To help plead the needs of the hour
Millions to be rescued from sin's bondage
As much still to grow to My image

Of those I called to look after the pews,
Not few looted my grace and forsook their posts
Serving riches and self with much boasts.
Would you bear My burden and Good News?

Remember soon I'll come like a thief;
Don't go to sleep by your selfish dreams.
Get back to me as quickly as it deems.
Hello, it's Jesus calling from the cliff.

No Match

There are strongholds;
But they are no match for our offensive Fold.
There are giants;
But they are dwarfed by our faith so robust and defiant
There are obvious barriers;
Easily surmountable are they by the Holy-Ghost-carriers!

REWARDS

Heavenly rewards...
They should be mostly esteemed
Than earthly awards
That's the desire of the Redeemed

We must serve faithfully
As God's stewards
Working dutifully
As though there are no awards

Claiming earthly accolade
Shouldn't be the drive
But that which wouldn't fade
The Joyful reward we derive

MY NOBLE VINE

How did you turn out this way?
You were of My choicest stock.
"I had planted you a noble vine
A seed of highest quality
How then have you turned before Me
Into the degenerate plant of an alien vine?"
(Jeremiah 2:21)

Under My searchlight, you were found
And founded, under My watch of grace
In My vineyard, you were watered
Before My eyes, I saw you grow and glow
You were my noble vine
How then did you turn out this way?

Like a degenerate plant, you have
Turned into a corrupt wild vine
Yet I planted you a seed of highest quality
Your once tender shoots now take the semblance
Of one of the other alien plants
What became of your root in the Lord?

Once you stood out in the world
As you stood up for My Word
Lifting the standard against opposing schemes
Now you nod to their modern disguises
Subtly compromising the Way
How did you turn out this way?

Have I laboured on you in vain?
Have my years of pruning come to waste?
What has become of you, My noble vine?
Have you lost the quality seed I planted?
Have you mingled with foreign wild vines?
Has the enemy grafted in you the strange plants?

Printed in the United States
By Bookmasters